Women in the American Revolution

Edited by Jeanne Munn Bracken

*Families of the Minutemen reluctantly sent their men off to battle.
(Drawing by Darley)*

Discovery Enterprises, Ltd.
Carlisle, Massachusetts

© Discovery Enterprises, Ltd., Carlisle, MA 1997

ISBN 1-878668-73-0 paperback edition
Library of Congress Catalog Card Number 96-84719

10   9   8   7   6   5   4   3

Printed in the United States of America

Subject Reference Guide:

Cataloging in Publication Data:

Women in the American Revolution Edited by Jeanne Munn Bracken.
Perspectives on History Series

I title
II Bracken, Jeanne Munn, editor
III Series

1. United States — History — Revolution, 1775-1783 — Women

2. United States — History — Revolution, 1775-1783 — Personal Narratives

3. Women — United States — History — Eighteenth Century

Dewey 973.3   Library of Congress E 276

Summary:
Colonial women did not have time to sit around weeping for their
men who were off fighting the Revolutionary War.
Here are some of their experiences: on the homefront, on the march,
in the line of danger, in camp, and "sneaking around."

Acknowledgments:

The author is grateful for the constant support and tireless fact-checking
of her colleagues throughout the reference community of the
Minuteman Library Network — especially Beverly Shank at Medford (MA);
Marcia Moss at Concord (MA); Susan Paju at Acton (MA); and never least,
the entire staff of the Lincoln Public Library and the Reuben Hoar Library
at Littleton (MA). The ever patient people at Discovery Enterprises, Ltd.,
especially JoAnne W. Deitch, deserve a tip of the author's (tricorner) hat as well.

Table of Contents

Dedication

Women in the American Revolution *is dedicated to my daughters,*
Lisa Jeanne Bracken and Mollie Howland Bracken —
descendants of good colonial stock.

The Women of the Revolution

by
Jeanne Munn Bracken

Source: Carl Holliday, *Woman's Life in Colonial Days*. Boston: Cornhill Publishing Company, 1922.

When I went home to my family in May, 1770 from the Town Meeting in Boston...I said to my wife, "I have accepted a seat in the House of Representatives, and thereby have consented to my own ruin, to your ruin, and to the ruin of our children. I give you this warning that you may prepare for your fate." She burst into tears, but instantly cried in a transport of magnanimity, "Well, I am willing in this cause to run all risks with you, and be ruined with you, if you are ruined." These were times, my friend, [wrote John Adams seventy years later to Benjamin Rush] in Boston which tried women's souls as well as men's.

War seems so masculine. The study of history usually involves learning, at various educational levels, about generals and battles, the dates, and perhaps, the military strategies. Except for Helen of Troy, who reportedly "caused" the Trojan War, or Joan of Arc, who led troops into battle, women are generally assumed to have been sitting back home, wringing their hands and worrying about the fate of their men — husbands, fathers, brothers, uncles, lovers.

Johnny Has Gone for a Soldier

A lovely and popular song, still sung today to the tune of the Irish lullaby "Shule Aroon."

Source: *Songs of Independence*, compiled and edited with historical notes by Irwin Silber. Harrisburg, PA: Stackpole Books, 1973, p. 87.

Here I sit on Buttermilk Hill
Who can blame me, cry my fill?
And ev'ry tear would turn a mill;
Since Johnny has gone for a soldier.

Me, oh my, I loved him so,
Broke my heart to see him go,
And only time will heal my woe,
Johnny has gone for a soldier.

I'll sell my rod, I'll sell my reel,
Likewise I'll sell my spinning wheel,
And buy my love a sword of steel,
Johnny has gone for a soldier.

I'll dye my dress, I'll dye it red,
And through the streets I'll beg for bread,
For the lad that I love from me has fled,
Johnny has gone for a soldier.

Whether or not sexism is the cause of this image of "Woman, pining away for her man at war," the notion is far from accurate. Women surely did worry about their men, but they had plenty to occupy their hands and their minds while they were about it.

For one thing, they were often forced to open their homes to soldiers and officers — sometimes on the same side in the conflict; sometimes not. They spent weeks, even months, cooking, cleaning, and caring for men whom they not only didn't know, but whose cause they often opposed.

There were also social duties. In one particularly elaborate fete, called the "Meschianza," women in Philadelphia partook of an elegant send-off for General Sir William Howe, who was returning to England. The event, in May of 1778, lasted for days, with parades, dancing, formal dinners, and fireworks. Meanwhile, the colonial troops were finishing their winter starving at Valley Forge a few miles away. Some women, especially in the South, were forced into hostessing and other social roles, but others, truth be told, probably welcomed a few moments of gaiety and a chance to dress up and enjoy themselves, even if the guest of honor was a Tory officer.

The vast majority of colonists lived in the countryside and the women, left behind — when the soldiers marched off to war — had sewing, cooking, baking, knitting, spinning, gardening, food preservation, animal care, butchering, and of course mothering to tend to; all of which likely left them very little idle time. Some ran businesses, such as taverns. Female printer, Katherine Goodard of Baltimore, published the first signed copy of the Declaration of Independence. Blacksmith Betsy Hagar helped repair weapons and cannon for the colonial army. Women living on remote farms even had to give up their homes, moving for safety to frontier stockades out of the reach of raiding Indians.

The women comforted the dying, nursed the sick and wounded, and raised funds for Washington's army, door-to-door. The Daughters of Liberty were less formally organized than their male counterparts in the Sons of Liberty, but they were active in the cause — promoting tea substitutes using flowers, fruit and herbs; extolling homespun wool rather than imported fabrics; and exerting peer pressure on neighbors to join boycotts of British goods — which sometimes ran to physical threats.

Fortunately, there have been several major efforts to collect information about these women and their sisters — our foremothers. This book attempts to highlight only a small portion of their stories. Rather than an exhaustive study of any single woman or political position, the intent is to show a variety of locations and experiences.

Instead of a strict chronological or geographical order, the material is arranged according to the situation in which the woman in question found herself — at home or away. Because the bulk of women did indeed stay home, their reminiscences make up the greater portion of this book.

War Clouds Gather

The Boston Massacre (which was actually a response to civilian harassment of British soldiers) and the Boston Tea Party are probably the most famous events leading up to the Revolutionary War. Elsewhere in the colonies, rebels were making impassioned speeches, gathering weapons and gunpowder, and steeling themselves and their families for the coming storm. Similar preparations were underway overseas as well, in anticipation of hostilities.

In Germany, the Baroness von Riedesel gathered her little family, a mountain of belongings, and a handful of servants, and followed her husband, a general of the Hessians who had been hired to help the British fight the colonists.

Although the women were not generally active in organizations leading up to the outbreak of war, their importance was not lost on the men who were.

Source: Frank Moore, *Songs and Ballads of the American Revolution*. Reprinted from a copy in the Barnard College Library, New York Times and Arno Press, 1969, pp. 48-50.

This song was printed in the *Boston News Letter* in 1769.

To the Ladies

Young ladies in town, and those that live round,
Let a friend at this season advise you;
Since money's so scarce, and times growing worse,
Strange things may soon hap and surprise you.

First, then, throw aside your topknots of pride;
Wear none but your own country linen;
Of economy boast, let your pride be the most
To show clothes of your own make and spinning.

What if homespun they say is not quite so gay
As brocades, yet be not in a passion,

For when once it is known this is much worn in town,
One and all will cry out — 'Tis the fashion!

And, one, all agree, that you'll not married be
To such as will wear London factory,
But at first sight refuse, tell 'em such you will choose
As enourage our own manufactory.

No more ribbons wear, nor in rich silks appear;
Love your country much better than fine things;
Begin without passion, 'twill soon be the fashion
To grace your smooth locks with a twine string....

A Colonial woman spinning yarn. (Library of Congress)

Although women didn't usually take an active part in the political speeches and rallies, they were particularly effective in one economic sense: as consumers, they were often instrumental in boycotting British goods. If they could slow shipping and cut profits, they might force English business interests to back a more supportive policy toward the colonies. This economic pressure couldn't be brought to bear without the cooperation and support of the women, and their actions kept the political arena simmering. Some of these boycotts worked better than others. Probably the best known was the campaign in Edenton, North Carolina, led by Penelope Barker, that rejected British tea and clothing. The "Edenton Compact" (October 1774) read:

The "Edenton Compact"

Source: Sally Smith Booth, *The Women of '76*. New York: Hastings House Publishers, 1973, pp. 12-14.

As we cannot be indifferent on any occasion that appears to affect the peace and happiness of our country...it is a duty that we owe not only to our near and dear relations and connections, but to ourselves who are essentially interested in their welfare, to do everything as far as lies in our power to testify our sincere adherance [to resolves made by the Province to boycott British goods] and we do therefore... subscribe this paper as a witness of our...solemn determination to do so.

The news of the Edenton ladies' determination reached London, where it was the subject of a political cartoon and much discussion that poked fun at the women. One Londoner wrote to his brother in the North Carolina colony:

I see by the newspapers the Edenton ladies have signalized themselves by the protest against tea drinking....Is there a female Congress at Edenton too? I hope not, for we Englishmen are afraid of the male Congress, but if the ladies...should attack us, the most fatal consequence is to be dreaded. So dextrous in the handling of a dart, each wound they give is mortal; whilst we, so unhappily formed by Nature, the more we strive to conquer them the more are conquered. The Edenton ladies, conscious I suppose of this superiority on their side...are willing, I imagine, to crush us to atoms...the only security on our side to prevent the impending ruin that I can perceive is the probability that there are few places in America which possess so much female artillery as in Edenton.

The Homefront

Most colonial women remained in their homes and on their farms, caring for their families as well as they could, and perhaps carrying on their husbands' and fathers' businesses as well. The war still caught up with many of them.

Source: Carl Holliday, *op. cit.*, pp. 303-304.

It required genuine courage to remain at home, often with no masculine protection whatever, with the ever-present danger of Indian raids, and there, with the little ones, wait and wait, hearing news only at long intervals, fearing even to receive it then lest it announce the death of the loved ones. No telegraph, no railroad, no postal service, no newspaper might offer relief, only the letter brought by some friend, or the bit of news told by some passing traveller. It was a time of agonizing anxiety....

These women faced actual dangers; for they were often near the firing line. John Quincy Adams says of his mother: 'For the space of twelve months my mother with her infant children dwelt, liable every hour of the day and the night to be butchered in cold blood, or taken and carried into Boston as hostages. My mother lived in...danger of being consumed with them all in a conflagration kindled by a torch in the same hands which on the 17th of June [1775] lighted the fires of Charlestown. I saw with my own eyes those fires, and heard Britannia's thunders in the Battle of Bunker Hill, and witnessed the tears of my mother and mingled them with my own.'

After the Battle of Bunker Hill, the British set fire to the town of Charlestown, burning homes and businesses alike.

Source: William W. Fowler, *Women on the American Frontier.* Hartford: S. S. Scranton & Co., 1882, pp. 124-125.

While the husbands and fathers...were on public duty the wives and daughters cheerfully assumed a large portion of the labor which women could perform. They assisted to plant, to make hay, to husk, and to garner the corn. The [rural] settlement was mainly dependent on its own resources for [gun] powder. To meet the necessary demand, the women boiled together a ley of wood-ashes, to which they added the earth scraped from beneath the floors of their house, and thus manufactured saltpeter, one of the most essential ingredients. Charcoal and sulphur were then mingled with it, and powder was produced "for the public defense...."

Each section of the country had its special burdens, trials and dangers. The populous districts bore the first brunt of the enemy's attack; the thinly settled regions were drained of men, and the women were left in a pitiable condition of weakness and isolation. This was largely the condition of Massachusetts and Connecticut, where nearly every family sent some, if not all, of its men to the war. In the South the patriots were forced to practice continual vigilance in consequence of the divided feeling upon the question of the propriety of separation from the mother-country. New York, New Jersey, and Pennsylvania were battle grounds, and here, perhaps more fully than elsewhere, were experienced war's woes and desolation. But in every State throughout the thirteen colonies, and in every town, hamlet, or household, where there were patriot wives, mothers or daughters, woman's claims to moral greatness in that crisis were gloriously vindicated.

Alphabet
For Little Masters and Misses 1775

In their patriotic fervor, they did not neglect the education of the children:

Source: Frank Moore, *op. cit.*, pp. 88-89.

A, stands for Americans, who scorn to be slaves;
B, for Boston, where fortitude their freedom saves;
C, stands for Congress, which, though loyal, will be free;
D, stands for defence, 'gainst force and tyranny.
    Stand firmly, A and Z,
    We swear for ever to be free!

E, stands for evils, which a civil war must bring;
F, stands for fate, dreadful to both people and king;
G, stands for George, may God give him wisdom and grace;
H, stands for hypocrite, who wears a double face.

J, stands for justice, which traitors in power defy,
K, stands for king, who should to such the axe apply;
L, stands for London, to its country ever true,
M, stands for *Mansfield*, who hath another view.

N, stands for *North*, who to the House the mandate brings,
O, stands for oaths, binding on subjects not on kings:
P, stands for people, who their freedom should defend,
Q, stands for quere, when will England's troubles end?

R, stands for rebels, not at Boston but at home,
S, stands for *Stuart*, sent by Whigs abroad to roam,
T, stands for Tories, who may try to bring them back,
V, stands for villains, who have well deserved the rack.

W, stands for *Wilkes*, who us from warrants saved,
Y, for York, the New, half corrupted, half enslaved,
Z, stands for Zero, but means the Tory minions,
Who threatens us with fire and sword, to bias our opinions.
    Stand firmly A and Z,
    We swear for ever to be free!

(See footnotes on words in italics on page 62)

"The Ladies Patriotic Song" encouraged women to inspire men to patriotism.

A Capture in Rhode Island

After a foray to New London, Connecticut, the British were determined to weaken the colonists before returning to New York. Tories, who sympathized with the British, were eager to identify their neighbors on the opposing side.

Source: Charles Carleton Coffin, *The Boys of '76: A History of the Battles of the Revolution.* New York: Harper and Brothers, Publishers, 1877, pp. 283-284.

In May, 1778, General Pigot, who was in command of the British in Newport, sent Lieutenant-colonel Campbell, with six hundred men, to burn some boats which the Americans were building at Warren. They sailed on a frigate and in boats. At daylight the people in Warren were astonished to find an army marching into town with drums beating and colors flying. The British burned the boats and the meeting-house, entered the houses, captured the citizens, and marched on to Bristol, burning twenty houses there, snatched rings from the fingers of the women, stole their silver shoe-buckles, pillaged the houses, and started back....

On the retreat through Warren, a drummer with a big base-drum fell behind. Some women, seeing that there were no troops near, seized whatever they could lay their hands on for weapons — brooms, shovels, and tongs — ran out, and surrounded him.

"You are our prisoner," they shouted.

"I am not sorry to be captured, for I am very tired," said the drummer, giving himself up.

Defending Her Property in New York

Women, left behind when their husbands and fathers went to war, had to guard their homes, farms and businesses, and keep them running as smoothly as possible — no matter what happened around them. In upstate New York, near Albany, Catherine Schuyler saw her husband march off to fight in the French and Indian War just a week after their wedding, so when the Revolutionary War visited at the nearby Battle of Saratoga, she was not afraid to defend her family's mansion with its heirlooms, which was in the path of the enemy soldiers.

Source: Carl Holliday, *ibid.*, pp. 309-310.

[Mrs. Schuyler] determined to save [family belongings], and back she hastened from town to country. As she pushed on, multitudes of refugees begged her to turn back; but no appeal, no warning moved her. It was mid-summer, and the fields were heavy with ripe grain. Realizing that this meant food for the invaders, she resolved to burn all....She ran into the midst of the waving stalks, tossed the flaming torches here and there, and for a moment watched the flames sweep through the year's harvest. Then, hurrying to the house, she gathered up her most valuable possessions, hastened away over the dangerous road, and reached Albany in safety.

Within a few hours [British General] Burgoyne and his officers were making merry in the great house, drinking the Schuyler wine, and on the following day the mansion was burned to the ground. But fate played the British leader a curious trick; for within a few days Burgoyne found himself defeated and a guest in the Schuyler home at Albany. "I expressed my regret," he has testified, "at the event which had happened and the reasons which had occasioned it. [Schuyler] desired me to think no more about it; said the occasion justified it, according to the rules and principles of war, and he should have done the same."

Burgoyne was extremely well received by Mrs. Schuyler and her little family. He was lodged in the best apartment in the house. An excellent supper was served him in the evening, the honors of which were done with so much grace that he was affected even to tears, and could not help saying with a deep sigh, "Indeed, this is doing too much for a man who has ravished their lands and burnt their home." Indeed, all through his stay in this house he and his staff of twenty were treated with the utmost courtesy by Catherine Schuyler.

A Hessian Admires the Women

Source: *Letters from America 1776-1779, being Letters of (German) Officers, with the British Armies during the Revolution*, translated by Ray W. Petterngill, Port Washington, NY: Kennikat Press, Inc. Repr. ed. [1964, c. 1924], pp. 116-120.

December 18, 1777

Friends, I am at Kenderhook [Kinderhook, NY] where I am due to treat the subject of pretty girls....The womenfolk in this whole extensive region way to Boston and New York are slender and straight, fleshy without being stout. They have pretty little feet, very solid hands and arms, and very white skin, and a healthy complexion, without having to paint. I have hardly seen one with pockmarks, but smallpox inoculation has long been in general use here. Their teeth are very white, their lips pretty, and their eyes very animated and laughing. At the same time they have natural good manners, a very unconstrained manner, a frank, gay face, and natural boldness. They think a great deal of cleanliness and of good footwear. They dress very decently....Thus dozens stood by the road everywhere and let us pass in review, laughed at us mockingly, or now and then roguishly extended an apple with a curtsy. We thought at first they were city girls...but lo! They were daughters of poor peasants....

We reached West Springfield [Massachusetts], a village or town with scattered houses and a church of its own; the

Connecticut [River] separates it from Oost [East] Springfield. They took us into their houses. The inhabitants were passable, but damned curious. From the village and all the neighborhood whole families with wives and daughters came marching in and went from house to house, in order, as they said, to have a look at the prisoners. Every one from the General down had to stand for this. The greater the rank, the longer and more attentively was one looked at. I was glad they were soon done with me, but my brigade commander had to endure more, no matter how sour a face he made. I offered the pretty girls chairs which they accepted, thus I gained time to get revenge by looking at them attentively in my turn. Finally we got heartily sick of the jest, for one party after another walked boldly into the room without even knocking. I almost believe our host charged admission....

...[in Brookfield, Massachusetts]...the inhabitants would not receive us into their houses; they maintained that neither the Congress, nor General Gates, nor Colonel Ried, who commanded our escort, could ask that of them....

...we had only a short march to Worcester, a thriving little city. After much discussion they received us into their houses and barns; von Baerner's battalion was put in a large meeting-house. I and my brigade commander lodged with a distinguished lady who has two sons in Howe's army and whose husband is staying in England. She is now living in her own house as tenant and has to pay the Committee annual rental on her furniture. To give her a quiet life, the Committee has her fields tilled and takes charge of the whole place. Lest anything be stolen, great padlocks have been put on her storehouses. This lady, whose condition touched our hearts, received us with genuine friendship and care. She has a very good education and her two very pretty daughters have patterned after her. We hesitated to accept all the little courtesies which the good lady tried to shower upon us, and had our own cooking done.

Captured by the Indians

Anna Oosterhout Myers (also Moyer) had as a child seen her parents, four sisters, and brother killed by Indians in the Mohawk Valley of New York colony. She and her remaining brother, taken captive by the Indians, were held for three years. One other brother, whose illness with whooping cough at the time frightened the Indians, was left alone. When she was a married woman, the Revolution brought war back to her.

Source: John C. Dann, ed., *The Revolution Remembered; Eyewitness Accounts of the War for Independence.* Chicago: The University of Chicago Press, 1980, pp. 271-274.

On Sunday, which was on the seventeenth day of April [1778], about sunrise in the morning and while some of [Anna's] children were sent a few rods from the house to feed some calves, this deponent discovered the horses...run past the door of the house greatly frightened, and at the same time she heard her children scream. She went to the door to see what was the matter and there saw several Indians who had taken the two children who had been sent out. ...One of the Indians was near the door when she went out, and he yelled and whooped and seized her by the arm. The Indians took her and her four children about fifty rods from the house and stopped. Soon after they stopped, they were met by another party of Indians who had been up to a neighbor's by the name of Christian Durt, who had [captured] the same Durt, his wife, and one child, and the said Henry Moyer [Anna's husband]. A few minutes before she had been taken by the Indians...her husband...had left the house and gone to the said Durt's to see about moving into the fort they had been building...and while there, was taken prisoner with the said Durt and his family.

She was discharged by the Indians soon after the parties met, as aforesaid, with a sucking child then about two years old. Her husband...and three of her children were then

White settlers feared Indian attacks. (Broadside from around 1800)

taken away by the Indians, and where they went she does not know except from information....She returned to her house, which she found rifled of such articles as the Indians could carry and set on fire. The Indians had put brands of fire between one or two beds, which were on fire when she returned. She succeeded in getting the beds out of the house and extinguished the fire and prevented the building from being entirely consumed. About two hours after the Indians left, two of her [daughters] returned, leaving...her husband and one of the children, a boy...then about three years old, prisoners with the Indians. When her daughters returned, they informed [Anna] that the Indians discharged them, and that their father also wanted the Indians to discharge the Boy...but they refused to do so and told...her husband that if he attempted to run away, they would kill his boy. The wife of said Durt was also discharged by the said Indians, and her husband and child, a boy about seven years old, were carried off by the Indians....

...her husband returned in the fall of 1779, having been absent more than a year and a half...and then returned to Fort Willett, where [Anna] was. [Their] son remained a prisoner with the Indians until peace was declared, when he returned home.

Anna's harrowing tale, told for the official record when she was probably in her eighties in 1840, succeeded in obtaining her a widow's pension based on her husband's subsequent service.

Women in Pennsylvania

After winning the Battle of Brandywine and taking a large number of colonists prisoner, the British pushed on toward Philadelphia. Washington's troops were poorly equipped and donations were sought from the citizens. Elizabeth Drinker, a Philadelphia Quaker, described the sight.

Source: Sally Smith Booth, *op. cit.*, p. 145.

Those men that collected Blankets, &c, in our ward, were this afternoon at each of our neighbors, but did not call upon us [because Quakers were pacifists]. It is reported, and gains credit, that ye English have actually crossed the Schuylkill, and are on their way towards us.

Many [citizens] have had their Horses taken from them this afternoon; some going one way, and some another. It is likely from ye present prospect of things that we shall have a noisy night, tho' at this time (9 o'clock), I hear nothing like it, but we, living back and retired, escape many hurries that others are exposed to. All ye Bells in ye city are Certainly taken away, and there is talk of Pump handles and Fire-Buckets being taken also—but that may be only conjecture. Things seem to be, upon ye whole, drawing towards great confusion.

Sally Wister, the teenaged daughter of a Philadelphia merchant, had left the city for safety in the countryside to go back to the city if the British were defeated. But the Americans were still retreating.

Source: *ibid.*, pp. 145-146.

Yesterday, which was the 24th of September [1777], two Virginia officers call'd at our house, and informed us that the British Army had cross'd the Schuylkill. Presently after, another person stopp'd, and confirmed what they had said ...thee may be sure we were sufficiently scared; however, the road was very still till evening.

About seven o'clock we heard a great noise. To the door we all went. A large number of waggons, with about three hundred of the Philadelphia Militia. They begged for drink, and several push'd into the house. One of those that entered was a little tipsy, and had a mind to be saucy.

I then thought it time for me to retreat; so I figured me (mightly scar'd as not having presence of mind enough to face so many of the military), running in at one door, and out another, all in a shake with fear; but after a while, seeing the officers appear gentlemanly, and the soldiers civil, I call'd reason to my aid. My fears were in some measure dispell'd, tho my teeth rattled and my hand shook like an aspen leaf.

Margaret Hill Morris was a Quaker, who helped both the Loyalists and Patriots during the occupation of her town, Burlington, New Jersey. (Library of Congress)

Some of General Howe's British army marched into Philadelphia, while others turned to face the colonists at Germantown. The Americans under Generals Sullivan and Greene, confused by fog, began shooting at each other by mistake and were lost. But Howe didn't take advantage of the colonists' retreat, heading for the comfort of Philadelphia to wait for supplies.

Source: *ibid.*, pp. 146-147.

As [Sally Wister] was lying in bed...Liddy came running into the room, and said there was the greatest drumming, fifing, and rattling of waggons that she had heard. What to make of this we were at a loss. We dress'd and down stairs in a hurry. Our wonders ceas'd.

...Sister Betsy and myself...went about half a mile from home, where we cou'd see the army pass....We made no great stay, but return'd with excellent appetites for our breakfast.

Several officers call'd to get some refreshment, but none of consequence till the afternoon. Cousin Prissa and myself were sitting at the door; I in a green skirt, dark short gown, &c. Two genteel men of the military order rode up to the door: "Your servant, Ladies" &c, and ask'd if they could have quarters for Gen'l Smallwood. Aunt Foulke thought she could accommodate them as well as most of her neighbors — said they would. One of the officers dismounted, and wrote SMALLWOODS QUARTERS over the door, which secured us from straggling soldiers. In the evening his Generalship came with six attendants, which compos'd his family, a large guard of soldiers, a number of horses and baggage-waggons. The yard and house were in confusion, and glitter'd with military equipment....

How new is our situation! I feel in good spirits, though surrounded by an army, the house full of officers, the yard alive with soldiers—very peaceable sort of men, tho'. They eat like other folks, talk like them, and behave themselves with elegance, so I will not be afraid of them, that I won't.

The fate of women whose husbands and fathers favored the British was left in the hands of the men who were victorious in the Revolutionary War. Elizabeth Graeme Ferguson was a wealthy Philadelphian living on her inherited estate near the city. Her husband, a poor Scotsman, sympathized with the British and served under General Howe as a commissary of prisoners.

Source: Lorenzo Sabine, *Biographical Sketches of Loyalists of the American Revolution with an Historical Essay*, new introduction by Ralph Adams Brown, vol. I., 1864. Reprint: Port Washington, NY: Kennikat Press, Inc. 1966, p. 421.

In 1778...Mrs. Ferguson made a long statement...in which she gave a narrative of [her husband's] conduct from September 1775 [when, as appears, he embarked for Bristol, England,] until her appeal...."As to my little estate," she remarked, "it is patrimonial [left to her by her father free and clear]...." In 1779 she appealed to the Council not to allow the sale of her property....The estate was, however, confiscated; but a part of it was restored to her by the Legislature in 1781. She separated from her husband, and died in 1801.

Women React to Looters in South Carolina

The Southern Colonies suffered in the war as much as the North did, although more of the famous battles and military campaigns took place in the North. Towards the end of the Revolution, Eliza Wilkinson, near Charleston, wrote a letter to a friend describing her experience with renegade looters.

Source: Sally Smith Booth, *op. cit.*, pp. 258-259.

I ventured to speak to the inhumane monster who had my clothes. I represented to him the times were such we could not replace what they'd taken from us, and begged him to spare me only a suit or two; but I got nothing but a curse for my pains; nay, so far as his callous heart from relenting, that, casting his eyes toward my shoes: "I want them buckles," said he, and immediately knelt at my feet to take them out, which, while he was busy about, a brother villain, whose enormous mouth extended from ear to ear, bawled out: "Shares there, I say; Shares." So they divided my buckles between them. The other wretches were employed in the same manner; they took my sister's ear-rings from her ears; hers, Miss Samuell's buckles; they demanded her ring from her finger...after bundling up all their booty, they mounted their horses. But such despicable figures! Each wretch's bosom stuffed so full, they appeared to be afflicted with some dropsical disorder....

After that batch of looters passed by, stragglers arrived to carry off whatever was left.

...We have been humbled to the dust, again plundered, worse than ever plundered! Our very doors and window shutters were taken from the house, and carried aboard the vessels which lay in the river opposite our habitation; the sashes beaten out; furniture demolished; goods carried off; beds ripped up; stock of every kind driven away; in short, distresses of every nature attended us.

As awful as Miss Wilkinson's situation, it could not compare to that of Eliza Lucas Pinckney. Eliza had, from the age of sixteen, managed her father's farms and estate and was one of the most successful businesswomen of the colonies and perhaps of all American women's history. She had been instrumental in developing the indigo (a dye plant) industry in the South, which for a time was even more important economically than cotton. By the time her husband died in 1758, she managed seven farms. The daughter and then the wife of British officers, she lived to see her sons help establish the new colonial government.

Her estates were so diminished by the end of the Revolution, through theft or destruction of her equipment and the desertion of slaves, that by the end of the war she couldn't pay off her debts.

Source: *ibid.*, p. 262.

It may seem strange that a single woman, accused of no crime, who had a fortune to live Genteely in any part of the world, that fortune too in different kinds of property, and in four or five different parts of the country, should in so short a time be entirely deprived of it as not to be able to pay a debt of under sixty pounds sterling, but such is my singular case. After the many losses I have met with, for the last three or four desolating years from fire, and plunder, both in Country and Town, I still had something to subsist upon, but alas the hand of power has deprived me of the greatest part of that, and accident the rest.

The labor of the slaves I had working at my son Charles' sequestered Estate...has not produced one farthing since the fall of Charles Town. Between thirty and forty head of tame cattle which I had on the same plantation...was taken last November...for the use of the army for which I received nothing.

My house in Ellory Street...which I immediately rented at one hundred per annum sterling, was in a short time after filled with Hessians, to the great detriment of the house and annoyance of the tenant, who would pay me no more for the time he was in it, than twelve guineas....

My plantation up the path, which I hired to Mr. Simpson for fifty guineas...was taken out of his possession and I am told Major Fraiser now has it for the use of the Cavalry, and Mr. Simpson does not seem inclined to pay me for the last half of the year 1781. To my regret and to the great prejudice of the place, the wood has also been all cut down for the use of the Garrison, for which I have not got a penny. The negroes I had in town are sometimes impressed [drafted for working] on the public works and make the fear of being so a pretence for doing nothing.... (1782)

A Frontier Woman Defends Herself

Women on the "frontier," in less populated and less protected rural areas, had to contend with soldiers on both sides of the Revolution, and often with Indians as well. Indian raids, which too often resulted in taking of captives, destruction of property, injuries, and death, took their toll on women who were just trying to live day-to-day. Experience Bozarth in Westmoreland County (Pittsburgh), Pennsylvania, found herself in the middle of such a raid in 1779.

Source: *ibid.*, pp. 193-194.

First, Experience used an axe on the head of one attacker:

...cutting out his brains. With these preliminaries completed, she...turned to this second Indian, and with her axe gave him several large cuts, some of which let his entrails appear. He bawled out: "Murder, Murder." On [hearing] this, sundry other Indians (who had hitherto been fully employed, hailing some children out of doors) came rushing in his relief; one of whose heads Mrs. Bozarth clove in two with her axe, as he stuck it in the door, which laid him flat upon the soil.

In the Fray

Deborah Sampson

The names of a few women have passed down through the centuries as those who, usually disguised as men, actually took to the battlefield against the British and their allies. Rather than teaching school, Deborah Sampson, disguised as "Timothy Thayer," joined the Continental Army for the same reasons most men did — for adventure and a change in her life. Discovered, she was sent away. Then in 1782, months after the surrender at Yorktown, she joined the 4th Massachusetts Regiment as Infantry Private Robert Shurtleff. She fought at West Point and was wounded at Tarrytown in New York, but her identity wasn't revealed until she fell ill with yellow fever and was hospitalized. Her doctor reportedly kept her secret and she was discharged a few weeks after the final peace treaty was signed in 1783. In later years, after marrying and bearing children, she went on the lecture circuit telling her remarkable story.

Deborah Sampson

Margaret Corbin

Margaret Corbin, on the other hand, followed the army for the same reason most women did: she went with her husband John to do camp chores. After he was fatally wounded by Hessian soldiers at the Battle of Harlem Heights (1776), she took over his place as an artillery gunner. She was wounded and never fully recovered; in July of 1779, she was the first woman to receive a pension from Congress.

Mrs. John Christian Shell

Even those women who didn't deliberately put themselves in the line of fire were often in danger. Following is the account of a Mrs. John Christian Shell.

Source: William W. Fowler, *op. cit.*, pp. 126-128.

Four or five miles north of the village of Herkimer, New York, stood the block-house of John Christian Shell, whose wife acted a heroic part when attacked by the Tories, in 1781. From two o'clock in the afternoon until twilight, the besieged kept up an almost incessant firing, Mrs. Shell loading the guns for her husband and older sons to discharge. During the siege, McDonald, the leader of the Tories, attempted to force the door with a crow-bar, and was shot in the leg, seized by Shell, and drawn within doors. Exasperated by this bold feat, the enemy soon attempted to carry the fortress by assault; five of them leaping upon the walls and thrusting their guns through the loop-holes. At that moment the cool courageous woman, Mrs. Shell, seized an axe, smote the barells, bent and spoiled them. The enemy soon after shouldered their guns, crooked barrels and all, and quickly buried themselves in the dense forest.

Molly Pitcher

Source: Richard Wheeler, *Voices of 1776*. New York: Thomas Y. Crowell Company, 1972.
Reprinted from *A Narrative of Some of the Adventures, Dangers and Sufferings of a Revolutionary Soldier* by Joseph Plumb Martin, Hallowell, Maine; 1830.

...Mary Ludwig Hayes, who was to go down in history as "Molly Pitcher" because, on this scorching day [at the Battle of Monmouth, June 28, 1778] she carried pitcher after pitcher of cool water for the artillerymen and the wounded. Martin noted that she also helped to serve one of the cannon.

Martin wrote: "While in the act of reaching a cartridge and having one of her feet as far before the other as she could step, a cannon shot from the enemy passed directly between her legs without doing any other damage than carrying away all the lower part of her petticoat. Looking at it with apparent unconcern, she observed that it was lucky it did not pass a little higher, for in that case it might have carried away something else, and continued her occupation."

Woman in the Enemy Camps: Baroness von Riedesel

Not all of those caught in the Revolutionary War were colonists. The British actually had more women in the camps with their soldiers, carrying out various chores, which was a boon for them. The Hessians, German soldiers hired by the British to help with the war, also sent women along. The most famous of these was the wife of General von Riedesel. Although a noblewoman — accustomed to finery and servants — in moments of greatest peril she shone. Her description of the events leading up to the Battle of Saratoga follows:

Source: Friederike Charlotte Luise von Massow, *Baroness von Riedesel and the American Revolution; Journal and Correspondence of a Tour of Duty*. A revised translation with introduction and notes by Marvin L. Brown, Jr. Published for the Institute of Early American History and Culture at Williamsburg, Virginia, by the University of North Carolina Press, Chapel Hill, 1965, pp. 54-63.

We had been warned to keep extremely quiet, fires were left burning everywhere, and many tents were left standing, so that the enemy would think the camp was still there. Thus we drove on all through the night. Little Frederika [*her maid's young daughter*] was very much frightened, often starting to cry, and I had to hold my handkerchief over her mouth to prevent our being discovered....

We spent the whole of the 9th [September 1777] in a terrible rainstorm, ready to march on at a moment's notice. ...My maid did nothing but bemoan her plight and tear her hair. I begged her to quiet herself, as otherwise she would be taken for a savage. Hereupon she became still more frantic, and she asked me whether I minded her behavior, and when I answered, "Yes," she tore off her hat, let her hair hang down over her face, and said, "It is easy for you to talk. You have your husband, but we have nothing except the prospect of being killed or of losing all we have." ...My other maid, my good Lena, although very much afraid, nevertheless said nothing.

Toward evening we finally reached Saratoga....The greatest misery and extreme disorder prevailed in the army. The commissary had forgotten to distribute the food supplies among the troops; there were cattle enough, but not a single one had been slaughtered. More than thirty officers came to me because they could stand the hunger no longer. I had coffee and tea made for them and divided among them all the supplies with which my carriage was always filled; for we had a cook with us who, though an arch-rogue, nevertheless always knew how to get hold of something for us and, as we learned later, often crossed streams at night in order to steal from the farmers sheep, chickens, and pigs, which he sold to us at a good price....

...in the afternoon we heard cannon and musketry again, and alarm and confusion prevailed. My husband sent me word to get immediately to a house which was not far away. I got into the [carriage] with my children, and just as we came up to the house I saw five or six men on the other side of the Hudson, who were aiming their guns at us. Almost involuntarily I thrust my children onto the floor of the [carriage] and threw myself over them. The same instant the fellows fired and shattered the arm of a poor English soldier behind me, who had already been wounded and was retiring into the house. Immediately after our arrival a terrifying cannonade began, which was directed principally at the house where we sought shelter, presumably because the enemy, seeing so many people fleeing thither, got the idea that the generals themselves were there. But, alas, the house contained only the wounded and women! We were finally forced to seek refuge in the cellar, where I found a place for myself and the children in a corner near the door. My children lay on the floor with their heads in my lap. And thus we spent the whole night. The horrible smell in the cellar, the weeping of the children, and even worse, my own fear prevented me from closing my eyes....

In the morning the Baroness, fearing an outbreak of illness, had everyone leave the cellar so it could be cleaned.

I examined our place of refuge; there were three fine cellars with well-vaulted ceilings. I suggested that the most seriously wounded men be put into one cellar, the women in another, and all the others in the third, which was nearest to the door. I had everything swept thoroughly and fumigated with vinegar, when, just as everyone was about to take his place, renewed, terrific cannon fire created another alarm...

I preferred staying near the door so that in case of fire I would be able to get out as quickly as possible. I had some straw put down, laid my bedclothes on it, and slept there with the children, with my serving women not far away.

Although the Baroness had her servants handy, she was hardly enjoying luxury as she organized the women (some of whom tended their dying husbands and others who had just become widows) and other noncombatants, all the while having to listen to the moans and cries of the wounded. And with her young children in her charge as well — surely she was a remarkable person.

My husband often wanted to send me to the Americans, in order to put me out of danger, but I told him it would be worse than anything I had had to bear heretofore to be with people with whom I should have to be polite while my husband was fighting them. He promised me, therefore, that I could continue to follow the army....

Our cook brought us food, but we had not water, and I was often obliged to quench my thirst with wine and even had to give the children some....

Because we were badly in need of water, we finally found the wife of one of the soldiers who was brave enough to go to the river to fetch some. This was a thing nobody wanted to risk doing, because the enemy shot every man in the head who went near the river. However, they did not hurt the woman out of respect for her sex, as they told us themselves afterwards....

One of the worst things we had to bear was the odor which came from the wounds when they began to fester....

On the other hand, not all the men who were with us deserved it. Some of them were cowards who had no reason whatever for staying in the cellar, and who later when we were taken prisoners, were well able to stand up in line and march. We were in this dreadful position six days....

Eventually the British and Hessians surrendered.

The good woman who had fetched water for us at the risk of her life now got her reward. Everyone threw a handful of money into her apron, and she received altogether more than twenty guineas. In moments like this the heart seems to overflow in gratitude.

On the March

While women in the eighteenth century were of course not as mobile as women today, it would be wrong to assume they just kept the home fires burning (an image, incidentally, much more valid then than now). For various reasons, they often found themselves on the road during the war — whether with troops or trying to escape them. Those ladies on the move came from every social level and from both political sides of the revolution.

Lady Agnes Frankland (Franklin), wife of Sir Charles Henry Frankland, had been a servant girl in a Marblehead [Massachusetts] tavern when she caught the eye of a British nobleman. Not unlike Henry Higgins of "My Fair Lady" fame, the Baronet took her to Boston, saw that she was educated, and made her his mistress— the difference in their social ranks creating a problem as regards marriage. After being miraculously saved in a Portuguese earthquake, he married Agnes, and they lived a fancy life in Europe until his death in 1765. She returned to America with her son, expecting to spend the rest of her life in her native land. The war, however, changed that.

Lady Frankland

Source: Lorenzo Sabine, *op. cit.*, p. 437.

Lady Frankland, accompanied by her natural son, arrived in America...in 1768. At Hopkinton [Mass.], May 1775; and alarmed at the movements of the people, her Ladyship asked leave to remove to Boston. The Committee of Safety gave her liberty to pass to the capital with six trunks, one chest, three beds and bedding for the same, six sheep, two pigs, one small keg of pickled tongues, some hay, three bags of corn, and other such goods as she should think proper to carry thither; and gave her a written permit accordingly....Thus protected, she set out on her journey with her attendants; but was arrested by a party of armed men, who detained her person and her effects, until an order for the release of both was ordained. To prevent further annoyance, the Provincial Congress furnished her with an escort; and...allowed her to take seven trunks, all her beds and bedding, all her boxes and crates, a basket of chickens, two barrels and a hamper, two horses and chaises, one phaeton, some ham and veal, and sundry small bundles; and required all persons who had any of her property in possession to place the same, essentially, at her disposal. The "arms and ammunition," deposited in a chaise, a committee retained....Lady Frankland was in Boston on the 17th of June and gazed from her own house upon the conflict on Bunker's Hill. She returned to England.

Jemima Warner

In the fall of 1775 Benedict Arnold led an army on an ill-fated attempt to capture Quebec, during which he was badly injured. Several women, including Jemima Warner (wife of one of the Pennsylvania troops) went on the expedition. From the start, the marchers were in trouble, badly supplied, slogging through swamps, dogged by illness, and hungry.

Source: Sally Smith Booth, *op. cit.,* pp. 50-52.

Our bill of fare for last night and this morning consisted of the jawbone of a swine destitute of any covering, reported Dr. Isaac Senter, a New Hampshire soldier on the march. Our greatest luxuries now consisted in a little water, stiffened with flour, in imitation of a shoemaker's paste....In company was a poor dog...which...was instantly devoured, without leaving any vestige of the sacrifice. Nor did the shaving soap...leather of their shoes, &c., share any better fate.

Jemima Warner had worse problems even than hunger. One day when the company stopped so stragglers could catch up, a teenaged Pennsylvania soldier (John Joseph Henry) reported later:

> There were two women attached to those companies, who arrived before we commenced the march. One was the...wife of a private of our company, a man who lagged on every occasion. These women having arrived, it was presumed that all our party were up. We were on the point of (continuing) when some one cried out, "Warner is not here." Another said he had sat down, sick, under a tree a few miles back. His wife begged us to wait a short time, and with tears of affection in her eyes, ran back to her husband. We tarried an hour. They came not.

Further back on the trail, a Connecticut man, Abner Stocking, saw what happened.

> My heart was ready to burst and my eyes to overflow with tears when I witnessed distress which I could not relieve. The circumstances of young [Warner] and his wife, who followed him through this fatiguing march, particularly excited my sensibility. They appeared to be much interested in each other's welfare and unwilling to be separated, but the husband, exhausted with fatigue and hunger fell victim to the King of terrors. His affectionate wife tarryed by him until he died, while the rest of the company proceeded on their way. Having no implements with which she could bury him she covered him with leaves, and then took his gun and other implements and left him with a heavy heart. After travelling 20 miles she came up with us.

Baroness von Riedesel

Baroness von Riedesel traveled thousands of miles in the course of the war, from her native Germany to England, where she was presented to the king; thence to America, where they ranged all up and down the East Coast from upstate New York to Charlottesville, Virginia — every mile by horse-drawn vehicles over rough roads during active hostilities. She was not forced to follow her husband but did so out of loyalty and a desire to care for him. Her account continues:

Source: Friederike Charlotte Luise von Massow, *op. cit.*, pp. 47-53.

When the army marched again...it was at first decided that I was to stay behind, but upon my urgent entreaty, as some of the other ladies had followed the army, I was likewise finally allowed to do so. We traveled only a short distance each day and were very often sorely tried, but nevertheless we were happy to be allowed to follow at all. I had the joy of seeing my husband every day. I had sent back the greater part of my luggage and had kept only a few of my summer clothes. Everything went well at first. We had high hopes of victory and of reaching the "promised land," and when we had crossed the Hudson and General Burgoyne said, "Britons never retreat," we were all in very high spirits.

...I had a large calash readied, with room for myself and the three children and my two maids; thus I followed the army right in the midst of the soldiers, who sang and were jolly, burning with the desire for victory. We passed through endless woods, and the country was magnificent, but completely deserted, as all the people had fled before and had gone to strengthen the American army....This was a great disadvantage for us, because every inhabitant is a born soldier and a good marksman; in addition, the thought of fighting for their country and for freedom made them braver than ever.

All this time my husband, like the rest of the army, had to stay in camp. I followed at about an hour's distance and visited my husband in camp every morning. Sometimes I had dinner with him in camp, but mostly he came to my place for dinner. The army made brief attacks every day, but none of them amounted to much. My poor husband, however, was unable to go to bed, or even undress a single night. As the weather was beginning to grow cool, Colonel Williams of the artillery, observing that our mutual visits were very fatiguing, offered to have a house with a chimney built for me for five to six guineas, where I could make my home. I accepted his offer, and the house, which was about twenty feet square and had a good fireplace, was begun. These houses are called log cabins....

Then the army moved on, and the Baroness' life became even more difficult.

On my way back to the house I met a number of savages [as she called the Indians] in war dress, carrying guns. When I asked them whither they were bound, they replied, "War! War!"...I was completely overwhelmed and had hardly returned to the house, when I heard firing which grew heavier and heavier until the noise was frightful. It was a terrible bombardment, and I was more dead than alive!

It was, in fact, the Battle of Saratoga, which was not a victory for the British and their allies.

...My husband took me aside and told me that things were going badly and that I must be ready to leave at any moment, but not to let anyone notice this. On the pretext, therefore, of wanting to move into my new house I had all my things packed.

One of the women with her, Lady Acland, learned that her husband had been badly wounded and taken prisoner; the Baroness also was with General Fraser, who died of his wounds before morning.

Wounded officers of our acquaintance kept arriving, and the bombardment was renewed again and again. There was talk of making a retreat, but no steps were taken in this direction. [Among the casualties of Saratoga was the Baroness' log cabin, which she never had a chance to enjoy.] Toward four o'clock in the afternoon I saw flames rising from the new house which had been built for me, so I knew that the enemy was not far away.

After the battle, when hundreds of British and Hessians had been taken prisoner, an observer wrote, with acceptable grammar and spelling of the time:

Source: Ronald Hoffman and Peter J. Albert, editors, *Women in the Age of the American Revolution*. Published for the United States Capitol Historical Society by the University Press of Virginia, Charlottesville, 1989, p. 15.

Great numbers of women, who seemd to be the beasts of burthen, having a bushel basket on their back, by which they were bent double, the contents seemd to be Pots and kettles, various sorts of Furniture, children peeping thro' gridirons and other utensils, some very young Infants who were born on the road, the women bare feet, cloathd in dirty raggs, such effluvia filld the air while they were passing, had they not been smoking all the time, I should have been apprehensive of being contaminated by them.

Ann Eliza Bleecker

Ann Eliza Bleecker, who lived near Albany, fled south through overgrown forests, carrying her four-year-old daughter and her baby Abella. A poet, she wrote of her flight from the British, her home lost, fearing the accompanying Indians more than Burgoyne's army. Before they reached safety, Ann came to understand that her younger daughter was on the brink of death.

Source: Sally Smith Booth, *op. cit.*, pp. 130-31.

"Written on the Retreat from Burgoyne"

Was it for this, with thee, a pleasing load,
I sadly wandered through the hostile wood —
When I thought Fortune's spite could do no more,
To see thee perish on a foreign shore?
Oh my loved babe! My treasures left behind
Ne'er sunk a cloud of grief upon my mind;
Rich in my children, on my arms I bore
My living treasures from the scalper's power;
When I sat down to rest beneath some shade,
On the soft grass how innocent she played,
While her sweet sister from the fragrant wild
Collects the flowers to please my precious child,
Unconscious of her danger, laughing roves,
Nor dreads the painted savages in the groves!

What thought my houses, lands, and goods are gone,
(My) babes remain—these I can call my own!
But soon my loved Abella hung her head —
From her soft cheek the bright carnation fled;
Her smooth transparent skin too plainly showed
How fierce through every vein the fever glowed.

Ann herself only lived to the age of thirty-one, mourning her child and the losses of the British invasion. Another unfortunate woman is better remembered today; Jane McCrea, engaged to a loyalist officer, was taken prisoner by Indians unaware that she was on the same side in the war. Arguing over an expected reward, the Indians began to fight amongst themselves and Jane was murdered, scalped, her belongings looted, and her body thrown into a ravine. The responsible Indian was reportedly pardoned by Burgoyne, but Jane's death was a rallying cry for many colonists who volunteered to fight with the Americans.

Sarah Osborn

Sarah Osborn had been a servant in Albany, New York, until she married a veteran, Aaron Osborn. Without consulting his wife, Aaron reenlisted and insisted that Sarah accompany him in his military service. Many years later she gave a deposition recalling her exploits during the Revolutionary War, and as far as they can be checked, her details are accurate. Luckily for historians, Sarah was a good observer with an excellent memory.

Source: John C. Dann, *op. cit.*, pp. 241-249.

...she was married to Aaron Osborn, who was a soldier during the Revolutionary War. That after (Sarah) had married said Osborn, he informed her that he was returned during the war, and that he desired (Sarah) to go with him.

Sarah refused until she was promised transportation either on horseback or in a supply wagon.

(Sarah), accompanied by her...husband and the same forces, returned...to West Point. (Sarah) recollects no other females in company but the wife of Lieutenant Forman and of Sargeant Lamberson. (Sarah) was well-acquainted with Captain Gregg and repeatedly saw the bare spot on his head where he had been scalped by the Indians. Captain Gregg had turns of being shattered in his mind and at such times would frequently say..."Sarah, did you ever see where I was scalped?" showing his head at the same time....She and her husband remained at West Point...for perhaps one year and a half. While at West Point, (Sarah) lived at Lt. Foot's, who kept a boardinghouse. (Sarah) was employed in washing and sew-

43

ing for the soldiers. Her said husband was employed about the camp. She well recollects the uproar occasioned when word came that a British officer had been taken as a spy. She understood at the time that Major Andre was brought up on the opposite of the river and kept there till he was executed....They [marched] to Philadelphia, (Sarah) on horseback through the streets, and arrived at a place towards the Schuylkill where the British had burnt some houses, where they encamped for the afternoon and night. Being out of bread, (Sarah) was employed in baking the afternoon and evening. (Sarah) recollects no females but Sergeant Lamberson's and Lieutenant Forman's wives and a colored woman by the name of Letta. The Quaker ladies who came round urged (Sarah) to stay behind, but her said husband said, "No..." Accordingly, next day they continued their march from day to day till they arrived in Baltimore, where (Sarah) and her husband..embarked on board a vessel and sailed down the Chesapeake.

General Clinton was in the same boat with her and Washington was apparently on one nearby, since she saw him when they got to Yorktown.

...Some of the troops went down by land. They continued sail until they had got up the St. James River as far as the tide would carry them. About twelve miles from the mouth, and then landed, and the tide being spent, they had a fine time catching sea lobsters, which they ate.

They, however, marched immediately for a place called Williamsburg...(Sarah) alternately on horseback and on foot. They...marched for Yorktown...(Sarah) was on foot....She saw a number of dead Negroes lying round their encampment, whom she understood the British had driven out of the town and left to starve, or were first starved and then thrown out. (Sarah) took her stand just back of the American tents, say about a mile from the town, and busied herself washing, mending, and cooking for the soldiers, in which she was assisted by the other females; some men washed their own clothing. She heard the roar of the artillery for a number of days...a misty foggy night, rather wet but not rainy...every soldier [built for himself] entrenchments. [Sarah's] said husand was there [building entrenchments] and she cooked and carried in beef, and bread, and coffee [in a gallon pot] to the soldiers in the entrenchment.

On one occasion when (Sarah) was thus employed carrying in provisions, she met General Washington, who asked her if she "was not afraid of the cannonballs?"

She replied, "No...that it would not do for the men to fight and starve, too."

The colonists built entrenchments closer and closer to Yorktown each night, the enemy firing all the time.

While digging...the enemy fired very heavy till about nine o'clock the next morning, then stopped, and the drums from the enemy beat excessively....

The drums continued beating, and all at once the officers hurrahed and swung their hats, and (Sarah) asked them, "What is the matter now?"

One of them replied, "Are you not soldier enough to know what it means?"

(Sarah) replied, "No."

They then replied, "The British have surrendered."

Sarah watched the British officers surrender, their fifes, decorated with black handkerchiefs, playing sad tunes. She and her husband stayed with the troops, moving back to New Jersey and then West Point, where they boarded some soldiers and helped local farmers. She had three children by Aaron, but he turned out to be a less than satisfactory husband. He had been intermittently absent and she discovered that he had another wife in Newburgh, New York. Aaron tried to make up to Sarah, but she tossed him out and never saw him again. She eventually married another war veteran, received pensions based on both of their service (although apparently her own was not recognized!) and lived to be upwards of one hundred years old.

Women in Camp

Much of war — as much of life — consists of waiting for something to happen. The women who had followed their husbands into the army were hardly idle bystanders. While General Washington had difficulty deciding if they were a boon for the work they performed or an additional drain on already scarce supplies, it is a fact that they were extremely useful. Men were not accustomed to mending their clothing, washing laundry, cooking, and many other day-to-day activities. These tasks the women performed, as they would have had they been at home. They served as nurses when the need arose, as it often did.

On the other hand, the women did require food and shelter, and they served as a reminder to the soldiers that there was another life, in another place — leading more than one to desert his company. The women did not fall under military discipline and caused problems as a result; also, they often carted their children along, adding more mouths to feed. (Children received half rations, but nursing babies were not allowed any). Most of the women in the camps were white, although in the South, black women could be found as well — usually slaves following their masters. If a slave had been enlisted in the place of his master, however, his wife would probably be kept on the home place as a near-hostage, a reassurance that he would not desert.

The women in the various military encampments had not necessarily found safety, either. One woman was killed, for example, in Arnold's camp outside Quebec when a soldier carelessly fired his loaded musket. For the most part, the women were appreciated.

Women at Valley Forge

Source: William F. Fowler, *op. cit.*, pp. 136-137.

The winter at Valley Forge was the darkest season in the Revolutionary struggle. The American army were sheltered by miserable huts, through which the rain and sleet found their way upon the wretched cots where the patriots slept. By day the half-famished soldiers in tattered (uniforms) wandered through their camp, and the snow showed the bloody tracks of their shoeless feet. Mutinous mutterings disturbed the sleep of Washington, and one dark, cold day, the soldiers at dusk were on the point of open revolt. Nature could endure no more, and not from want of patriotism, but from want of food and clothes, the patriotic cause seemed likely to fail. Pinched with cold and wasted with hunger, the soldiers pined beside their dying camp-fires. Suddenly a shout was heard from the sentinels who paced the outer lines, and at the same time a cavalcade came slowly through the snow up the valley. Ten women in carts, each cart drawn by ten pairs of oxen, and bearing tons of meal and other supplies, passed through the lines amid cheers that rent the air. Those devoted women had preserved the army, and Independence from that day was assured.

Mrs. Washington in Camp

Source: Rev. Edward C. Jones, *'76, Lyrics of the Revolution.* Philadelphia, privately published 1899, pp. 105-106.

Mrs. Martha Washington was accustomed to say that, owing to her yearly residences in the camp during the winter season, she had heard the first cannon at the opening and the last at the closing of all the campaigns in the Revolution.

She heard the opening peal
　　Which ushered in the fray,
When first on Cambridge's noble heights
　　The stern encampment lay;
From blue Potomac's flood,
　　From home and its employ,
She travelled with a woman's zeal
　　To prove her hero's joy.

When weary men and worn
　　At Morristown were placed,
And on their leader's troubled brow
　　Sorrow its mark had traced,
New Jersey's heart her image held
　　In its recesses warm.

When Pestilence his wing
　　O'er Valley Forge had spread,
The gentle wife was there, amid
　　The dying and the dead,
And benisons fell thick
　　Where'ere her footsteps moved;
She was the idol of the camp,
　　Whose simple name they loved.

Source: Carl Holliday, *op. cit.*, pp. 135-136.

Hear the description of Mrs. Washington as given by one of the ladies at the camp of Morristown (NJ, 1779); — with what simplicity of manner the first lady of the land aided in a time of distress:

"Well, I will honestly tell you, I never was so ashamed in all my life. You see, (we three wives) thought we would visit Lady Washington, and as she was said to be so grand a lady, we thought we must put on our best bibbs and bands.

Martha Washington

So we dressed ourselfes [sic] in our most elegant ruffles and silks, and were introdced to her ladyship. And don't you think we found her knitting *and with a (check) apron on*! She received us very graciously, and easily, but after the compliments were over, she resumed her knitting. There we were without a stitch of work, and sitting in State, but General Washington's lady with her own hands was knitting stockings for herself and husband!

"And that was not all. In the afternoon her ladyship took occasion to say, in a way that we could not be offended at, that it was very important, at this time, that American ladies should be patterns of industry to their country-women, because the separation from the mother country will dry up the sources whence many of our comforts have been derived. We must become independent by our determination to do without what we cannot make ourselves. Whilst our husbands and brothers are examples of patriotism, we must be patterns of industry."

Mrs. Coughlan

The British and their allies also had women in camp, perhaps even including escaped black slaves. Some of the women were the widowed or deserted wives of the German Hessian troops, who, unable to speak English, were less likely to take up with the British soldiers on any permanent basis.

Mrs. Coughlan, daughter of an aide to General Monchton, was born in Nova Scotia, sent to Dublin at the age of three for education, returned to New York in 1772, and married a British soldier. Her published memoirs include eyewitness accounts of not only the American Revolution but also the French Revolution, in which she found herself embroiled a few years later.

Source: *Memoirs of Mrs. Coughlan, Daughter of the Late Major Moncrieffe Written by herself with Introduction and Notes.* New York: T. H. Morrell, 1864, reprint ed. Later reissued in the Arno Press series "Eyewitness Accounts of the American Revolution", 1971, pp. 37-39.

The success of the Royalists soon restored to us the possession of our property at New York, where we were no sooner settled, than my father sent an invitation to the widow of a gentlemen...requesting her to accept his house as an assylum; his object in so doing was on my account, his public situation obliging him to be ever absent from home. — I had now acquired a number of admirers; but having positively *renounced* all thoughts of *marriage*, I obtained consent to depart for England with Colonel and Mrs. Horsfall, who were to embark in the Month of March, 1777. It was then resolved that, on my arrival in England, I should be placed at...boarding-school. — How vain is it for mortals to anticipate plans which Providence in an instant can entirely destroy!

Mr. Coughlan, my present husband, saw me at an assembly, when without either consulting *my heart*, or deigning to ask my permission, he instantly demanded me in marriage, and won my father to his purpose.

Although she was vocally opposed to the match, her father approved, and that sealed her fate. It was a disastrous marriage, allowed by her father with her safety in mind. While her husband was handsome and wealthy, he was of poor character. The pair eventually sailed for Ireland in early 1778.

Baroness von Riedesel "on duty"

In June of 1778 the Baroness von Riedesel and her family were encamped, captives, at Cambridge, Massachusetts.

Source: *Memoirs and letters and journals of Major General Riedesel, during his residence in America.* J. Munsell, 1868, translated by William L. Stone, two volumes, pp. 28-9, 84-87.

On the 14th (of June) a new difficulty arose between the provincials and a (Hessian) soldier...which cost him later his life. He was on the point of going beyond (the boundary) with his young and beautiful wife who had followed him from Europe, when six brutal militia men began joking with the woman in a coarse manner. The husband in protecting the honor of his wife finally found himself forced to defend her and himself with a cane against their assailants. The sentinel near by, witnessed the unequal combat with all composure, but when the German drove back the Americans, he ran up and thrust his bayonet through him. The poor man soon expired. Riedesel...complained bitterly...whereupon... the murderer (was sent) to Boston for trial; but it could never be ascertained what was done to him.

In early 1780, by then in New York, the Riedesels welcomed a new daughter, named America.

A few days subsequent to the baptism, his eldest daughter was taken dangerously sick and, shortly after, the third one, Caroline, also fell seriously ill. General Riedesel, who loved his family dearly, became, in consequence, very much alarmed, and being already greatly depressed, he fell into a state of melancholy hypochondria. It can, therefore, readily be seen that his wife had her hands full, not only in taking care of her sick children — both of whom shared her bed — but in cheering and comforting her husband. Fortunately her naturally joyous temperament enabled her to bear these misfortunes easily....

This was not the Baroness' only nursing experience during the war. Even on the ship to America years before, she had been the only one healthy enough to care for the others, who were all dreadfully seasick. Then, later, while they were guests of General Clinton in the Hudson Valley, they became ill again.

The pleasant visit at (General) Clinton's villa was clouded by the malignant fevers which, in that country, are frequent in this season of year, but which were even worse during the present year than usual. At one time all the family of Riedesel, including the servants, were sick with the exception of his wife, the pastor... and the faithful (footman) Rockel [who had travelled from Germany with Mrs. Riedesel and her daughters]. The general, his little daughter Augusta, and six of his (servants) were at one time at death's door. Indeed, at one period, during his illness, the (general) cared little whether he lived or died; for in addition to the fever he was attacked with a disease resembling cholera, which brought him very low. His powerful constitution, however, aided by the care of a skillful physician from New York, enabled him to conquer this severe attack. Mrs. Riedesel had the entire care of this hospital, besides nursing a little infant; yet she managed to attend to the comfort of all the invalids. Day and night she ministered to the wants of her husband and servants, and neglected not the child. During the whole of this time she never undressed, but threw herself upon the bed ready to respond at a moment's notice to the call of the sick. In a word, she was the same angel that ministered to the wounded during the days of terror at Saratoga. A kind providence repaid her for her self-sacrifice; and she had the happiness of seeing her husband, her child and her servants fully restored to health.

Mrs. Slocum Seeks Her Husband

In the American South, fewer major battles were fought but often smaller skirmishes engulfed local folks. Mrs. Slocum, from Pleasant Green, North Carolina, grew tired of waiting for her husband to come home from a meeting with the British, and felt compelled to go after him.

Source: Sally Smith Booth, *op. cit.*, pp. 248-249.

The cool night seemed after a gallop of a mile or two, to bring reflection with it, and I asked myself where I was going and for what purpose. Again and again I was tempted to turn back; but I was soon ten miles from home, and my mind became stronger every mile I rode that I should find my husand dead or dying....When day broke I was some thirty miles from home, I knew the general route our army expected to take, and had followed them without hesitation. About sunrise I came upon a group of women and children, standing and sitting by the road-side, each one of them showing the same anxiety of mind which I felt.

Stopping for a few minutes I inquired if the battle had been fought. They knew nothing, but were assembled on the road-side to catch intelligence.

The sun must have been well up, say eight or nine o'clock, when I heard a sound like thunder, which I knew must be cannon. It was the first time I ever heard a cannon. I stopped still; when presently the cannon thundered again. The battle was then fighting!

Following the sound, she soon came upon twenty men who had been wounded. Among them was a badly injured man whom she thought was her husband.

I remember uncovering his head and seeing a face crusted with gore from a dreadful wound across the temple. I put my hand on the bloody face; 'twas warm; and an unknown voice begged for water. ...it was not my husband but Frank Cogdell....A Puddle of blood was standing on the ground about his feet. I took the knife, and cut away his trousers and stockings and found the blood came from a shot hole through and through the fleshy part of his leg. I looked about and could see nothing that looked as if it would do for dressing wounds, but some heart-leaves. I gathered a handful and bound them tight on the holes; and the bleeding stopped. I then went to others....

She nursed both American and enemy soldiers, begged for mercy for captured Tories, and finally found her husband, "bloody as a butcher, and as muddy as a ditcher..." and unwounded. She returned home.

Spies, Smugglers and "Sneaks"

Some of the most famous women of the Revolution were spies; others undertook dangerous missions to supply the colonial army with information or materials. In Philadelphia, Lydia Darragh has attained the status of legend for reportedly stealing out of her house (occupied by top British commanders) to carry a warning of an impending strike; while her exploits are of questionable historic accuracy, they certainly could have happened. At any rate, Mrs. Darragh was a respected businesswoman who left a sizable estate.

Two other women whose deeds during the war are still argued to this day are Margaret Kemble Gage, the wife of General Thomas Gage of Lexington and Concord fame, and Peggy Shippen Arnold, wife of Benedict. In the former's case, the general afterward insisted he had told only one person of his intentions to send troops into the countryside, and that was his wife (an American by birth). Some have suspected that she passed the word to rebels and thus sealed the fate of the marching Redcoats — and, ultimately, of Boston.

Scholars still debate today whether Peggy Arnold knew of her husband's treachery before he was caught. A high-living, vivacious lady, she was expensive to maintain and Arnold might have been tempted more by the money he would receive for his intelligence operation than by politics (although he did feel that his military exploits were not recognized with sufficient career advancement). When she was told of Benedict's arrest, Peggy put on an impressive show of shock and grief. Her husband —said she— was innocent; but history still has not decided if she was a bystander or the instigator of the treason.

Elsewhere other women, less famous today, were risking their lives for their cause. In Charleston, South Carolina, which was British-occupied and under siege in 1779, women smuggled food and supplies to the rebels. Their system worked pretty well for a while — until a sharp-eyed British official noticed that women leaving the city were slim, but upon returning a short time later they had bulging clothing. Searches carried out by Loyalist spinsters soon put an end to this trickery.

Deborah Champion Carries Dispatches

In New England in early 1776, the Americans were holding the British in Boston. Within the city, food and other supplies were growing scarce. Under Washington's new leadership, fresh troops had been recruited to replace those who had already completed their short enlistments. In Connecticut, young Deborah Champion, daughter of an American Colonel, was asked to carry vital dispatches to Washington, in the belief that the twenty-two-year-old woman would seem less suspicious to wandering British guards. In the company of a servant, she set off. Her account follows:

Source: Sally Smith Booth, *op. cit.*, pp. 55-57.

Early in the morning, before it was fairly light, mother called me, though I had seemed to have hardly slept at all....Father told me again of the haste with which I must ride and the care to use for the safety of the dispatches, and I set forth on my journey with a light heart and my father's blessing.

The British were at Providence, in Rhode Island, so it was thought best I should ride due north to the Massachusetts line, and then east as best I could to Boston. The weather was perfect, but the roads none too good as there had been recent rains, but we made fairly good time going through Norwich, then up the Valley of the Quinebaug to Canterbury, where we rested our horses for an hour, then pushed on, hoping to get to Pomfret before dark. All went as well as I could expect. We met few people on the road, almost all men being with the army and only the very old men and the women at work in the villages and farms. Dear heart, but war is a cruel thing!

I heard that it would be almost impossible to avoid the British unless by going so far out of the way that too much time would be lost, so I plucked up what courage I could and secreting my papers in a small pocket in the saddlebags, under all the eatables mother had filled them with, I rode on, determined to ride all night. It was late at night, or rather very early in the morning, that I heard the call of the sentry and knew that now, if at all, the danger point was reached, but pulling my (bonnet) still farther over my face, I went on with what boldness I could muster. Suddenly I was ordered to halt; as I couldn't help myself, I did so. I could almost hear (my servant's) teeth rattle in his mouth, but I knew he would obey my instructions and if I was detained would try to find the way alone. A soldier in a red coat proceeded to take me to headquarters, but I told him it was early to wake the captain, and to please to let me pass for I had been sent in urgent haste to see a friend in need, which was true if ambiguous. To my joy, he let me go, saying, "Well, you are only an old woman anyway," evidently as glad to get rid of me as I of him.

Deborah completed her ride to Boston safely, and on March 17, 1776, the British left the port city of Massachusetts for the last time.

Mrs. Murray Entertains the Enemy

In September 1776, after British General Howe's smashing defeat of the Americans under General Putnam at the Battle of Long Island, the colonial army was in retreat with the enemy hot on their heels, barely two miles behind them.

Source: Charles Carleton Coffin, *op. cit.*, pp. 109-110.

General Washington sent a message to Putnam. "Escape immediately," was the order.

The only way of escape left open was up the shore of the Hudson, along cart-paths, for the British were already in possession of the Boston road.

General Putnam did not know the way, but, fortunately, he had a young officer for an aid who knew every path and by-way—the officer...Aaron Burr. General Putnam started.

There was one brigade...in a little fort which the Americans had named Bunker Hill (corner of Broadway and Grand Street). Major Burr rode up to it.

"Why are you lingering here for? Why don't you retreat?" he shouted.

"We can not retreat. The British have possession of the road! We will stay here and hold the fort," said General Knox.

"You can't hold it ten minutes. You have no water, no provisions. There is no place where the troops can be sheltered from the bombs. The British will throw in shells and make it a slaughter-pen," said Burr.

"It will be madness to attempt to retreat," Knox replied.

"I can guide you. I know every cow-path."

They trusted him, and went upon the run, down through the fields to the Hudson...then through woods, along narrow paths, and so escaped.

Just about the time that General Putnam started, (British Generals) Howe and Clinton, having compelled Washington to retreat, rode west half way to the Hudson, and drew up at the house of Mr. Murray. It was a delightful mansion with a lawn and graveled walks in front, a green-house, and rustic seats. Mrs. (Mary L.) Murray received them courteously, and it occurred to her that if she could entertain them a while it might be of some service to General Washington. She invited them in, told the servants to prepare a lunch, and entertained them so charmingly that they forgot all about affairs outside. She kept them fully two hours; and while they were sipping Mrs. Murray's wine, and listening to her engaging conversation, General Putnam, with his four thousand men, was slipping past them not a half mile away.

General Howe was greatly chagrined when he learned that Putnam had escaped.

Whatever the reason that the British lingered at Mrs. Murray's table, the stage was now set for Washington to push back the British at the Battle of Harlem Heights.

Dicey Langston Warns of Danger

To the South, other women were as active — and as "sneaky."

Source: William W. Fowler, *op. cit.*, pp. 127-8, 139.

Dicey Langston, of South Carolina, also showed a "soul of love and bravery." Living in a frontier settlement, and in the midst of Tories, and being patriotically inquisitive, she often learned by accident, or discovered by strategy, the plottings so common in those days against the Whigs. Such intelligence she was accustomed to communicate to the friends of freedom on the opposite side of the Ennosee river.

Learning one time that a band of loyalists — known in those days as the "Bloody Scouts" — were about to fall upon the "Elder Settlement," a place where a brother of hers and other friends were residing, she resolved to warn them of their danger. To do this she must hazard her own life. Regardless of danger she started off alone, in the darkness of the night; traveled some miles through the woods...came then to...a rapid and deep stream, into which she plunged and waded till the water was up to her neck. She then became bewildered, and zigzagged the channel for some time, finally reaching the opposite shore....She then hastened on, reached the settlement, and her brother and the whole community were saved....

Mrs. Richardson Helps the Cause

...While the conflict was at its height in South Carolina, Captain Richardson, of Sumter district, was obliged to conceal himself for a while in the thickets of the Santee swamp. One day he ventured to visit his family — a perilous movement, for the British had offered a reward for his apprehension, and patrolling parties were almost constantly in search of him. Before his visit was ended a small party of soldiers presented themselves in front of the house. Just as they were entering, with a great deal of composure and presence of mind, Mrs. Richardson appeared at the door, and found so much to do there at the moment, as to make it inconvenient to leave room for the uninvited guests to enter. She was so calm, and appeared to unconcerned, that they did not mistrust the cause of her wonderful diligence, till her husband had rushed out of the back door, and safely reached the neighboring swamp.

Emily Geiger Acts as a Courier

Another Southern woman courier was Emily Geiger.

At length Emily Geiger presented herself to General Greene, and proposed to act as his messenger; and the general, both surprised and delighted, (agreed) with her proposal. He accordingly wrote a letter and delivered it, and at the same time communicated the contents of it verbally, to be told to Sumter in case of accidents.

She pursued her journey on horseback, and on the second day was intercepted by (enemy) scouts. Coming from the direction of Greene's army and not being able to tell an untruth without blushing, Emily was suspected and confined to a room; and the officer sent for an old Tory matron to search for papers upon her person. Emily was not wanting in expedients, and as soon as the door was closed and the bustle a little subsided, she ate up the letter, piece by piece. After a while the matron arrived, and upon searching carefully, nothing was found of a suspicious nature about the prisoner, and she would disclose nothing. Suspicion being then allayed, the officer commanding the scouts suffered Emily to depart. She then took a route somewhat circuitous to avoid further detentions and soon after struck into the road leading to Sumter's camp, where she arrived in safety. Emily told her adventure, and delivered Greene's verbal message to Sumter, who in consequence, soon after joined the main army at Orangeburgh.

Peace

General Cornwallis surrendered his troops at Yorktown, Virginia, on October 19, 1781. The fate of the British was sealed, but scattered hostilities continued until Congress formally declared the war ended on April 11, 1783. News of the Yorktown victory reached Philadelphia on October 22 and two days later the city celebrated with a grand illumination. The pacifist Quakers, however, chose not to participate in the festivities and were singled out by mobs for ridicule.

Source: Elaine Forman Crane, ed., *The Diary of Elizabeth Drinker, The Life Cycle of an Eighteenth-Century Woman.* Boston: Northeastern University Press, 1994, pp. 91-92.

...the 17th of this month Octor. Genl Cornwallace (sic) was taken; for which we (Quakers) greviously suffer'd on the 24th by way of rejoyceing — a mobb assembled about 7 o'clock or before, and continud their insults until near 10; to those whose Houses were not illuminated scarcely one Friends House escaped we had near 70 panes of Glass broken the sash lights and two panes of the front parlor broke in pieces — the Door crack'd and Violently burst open, when they threw Stones into the House for some time but did not enter — some far(e)d better and some worse — some Houses after braking the door they enterd, and distroy'd the furniture & c. — many women and Children were frightend into fits, and 'tis a mercy no lives were lost.

Hundreds of miles to the northeast of Philadelphia, another woman was grateful for the end of the war, but also concerned about the politics of the new country. Writing to her husband John, Abigail Adams advised:

In the new code of laws which I suppose it will be necessary for you to make, I desire you would remember the ladies and be more generous and favorable to them than your ancestors.

Footnotes to Alphabet

North — Lord North was British prime minister a the time of the Revolution, the guiding force behind the Intolerable Acts.

Wilkes — John Wilkes, an English politician who opposed George III on the subject of the American colonies, successfully sued the royal government for illegal arrest. In so doing, he established the legal principle that general warrants are unconstitutional.

Stuart — John Stuart, the 3d Earl of Bute, as prime minister made the unpopular Treaty of Paris with France and Spain that ended the French and Indian War in 1763.

Mansfield — William Murray, 1st Earl of Mansfield, was a British judge who ruled that a Virginia slave who reached England and sought freedom there could not be forcibly removed to the colony for punishment.

Suggested Further Reading

All of the materials used in preparation of this book would be excellent sources for further research. In particular I would recommend:

Booth, Sally Smith. *The Women of '76*. New York: Hastings House Publishers, 1973.

> *A well-written, interesting examination of the roles played by women in this period of history. For high school and older readers.*

Kerber, Linda K. " 'History can do it no justice,' Women and the reinterpretation of the American Revolution." In: *Women in the Age of the American Revolution*, edited by Ronald Hoffman and Peter J. Albert. Charlottesville, VA: University Press of Virginia, 1989.

> *A thought-provoking examination for older readers, this essay shows how the roles of colonial women have been differently interpreted depending on the historian studying the issue.*

In addition, the following provide solid background information:

Salmon, Marylynn. *The Limits of Independence; American Women 1760-1800*. The Young Oxford History of Women in the United States, vol. 3. New York: Oxford University Press, 1994.

> *Well-illustrated and useful for middle readers on up.*

Zeinert, Karen. *Those Remarkable Women of the American Revolution*. Brookfield, CT: Millbrook Press, 1996.

> *A well-reviewed new source for middle readers.*

Zell, Fran. *A Multicultural Portrait of the American Revolution*. New York: Benchmark Books/Marshall Cavendish, 1996.

> *Another well-illustrated discussion, not only of women but of various racial and ethnic groups. Juvenile reading level.*

About the Editor

Jeanne Munn Bracken, whose maternal grandmother was a member of the Daughters of the American Revolution, is a freelance writer and a reference librarian. In the *Perspectives on History Series*, she has also edited books on the beginnings of the Revolution, life in the colonies, the transcontinental railroad, and the orphan trains that rumbled over the rails into America's heartland. Her other books are a reference guide for the parents of children with cancer and a corporate history. Her articles, reviews, and commentaries have appeared in magazines and newspapers from coast-to-coast. Jeanne lives in Massachusetts with her husband, two daughters, and several pets. She is reference librarian in Lincoln, Massachusetts, where revolutionary history is carried on the very wind.